A To Z
PositiveMindset

by

Helena Callaghan

A is for AMAZING. Say it out loud "I am Amazing" or "I am Awesome"!". Affirmations are a great way to start your day in a positive way. Repeat them every morning in the mirror (in your mind or out loud) before or after you brush your teeth. Or you can do them any time you like!

B

B is for BELIEF. Believe in your goals and dreams. You can do anything you put your mind to. B is also for BREATH – Deep breath in deep breath out. Repeat three times.

Believe

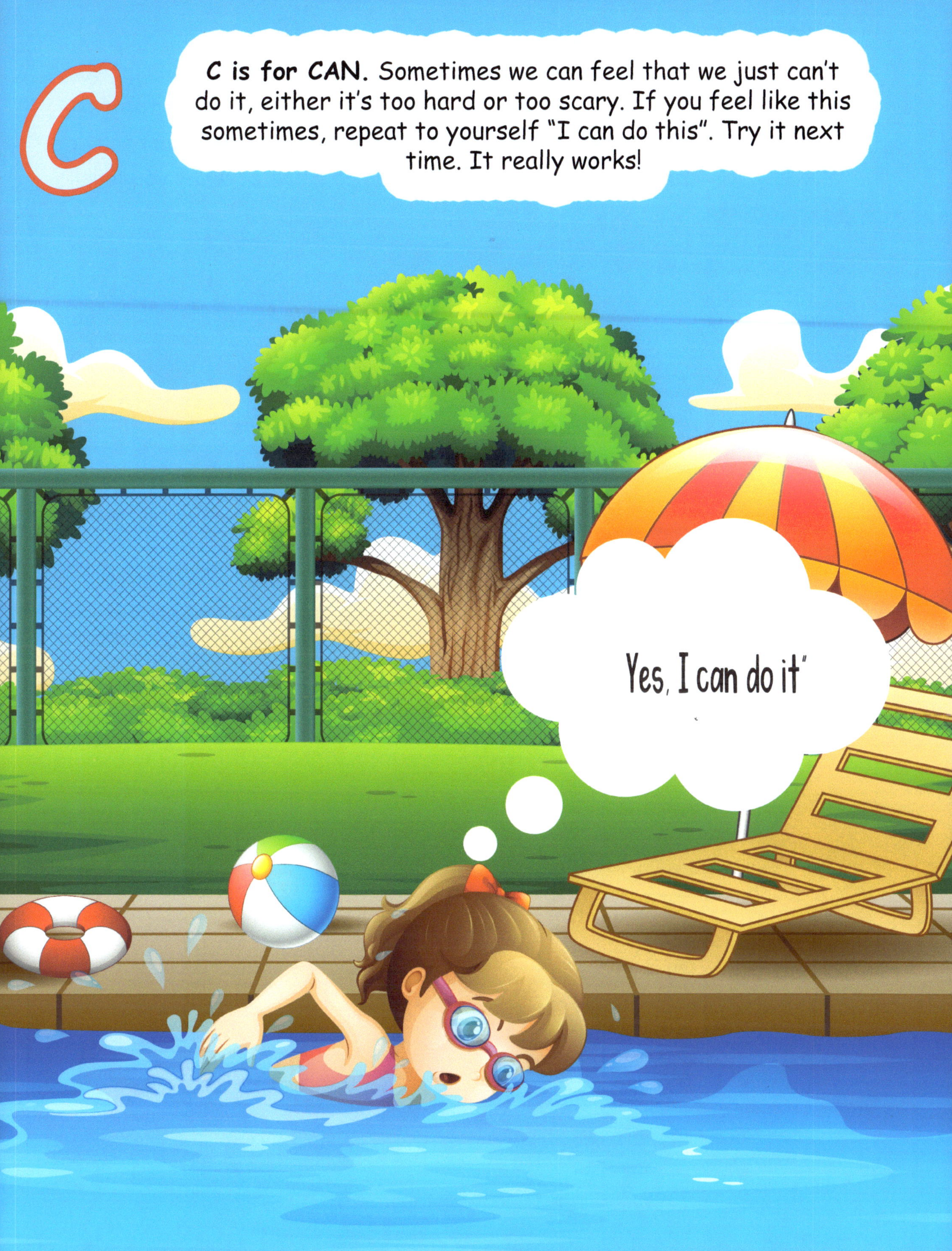

C is for CAN. Sometimes we can feel that we just can't do it, either it's too hard or too scary. If you feel like this sometimes, repeat to yourself "I can do this". Try it next time. It really works!

C

Yes, I can do it"

D
D is for DREAM. Dream big, let your imagination run wild. Imagine what you would love your life to look like in the future. Concentrate on it every day and you know - dreams really do come true. D is also for DO. Do more of what you love!

E
E is for EFFORT. Try to give 100% to everything you do! Even if it seems hard, all you can do is try your best. So make sure to give every task your absolute best effort.

F
F is for FUN. Have fun! Be yourself! Having fun makes life so much better! Laugh and be happy! F is also for FRIENDS. Who are your friends? Do you have fun with your friends?
SCHOOL

G
G is for GRATITUDE. Every night before you go to sleep say thank you to the Universe! Just pick one thing every day. It could be "Thank you for my food today" or "Thank you for my warm cosy bed.

H is for HAPPINESS. Don't worry, be happy!
Happiness is contagious! Everybody can feel it from you!
H is also for HUGS! Hug someone you love today!

I
I is also for "I". Hey! I am talking to you! You are the most important person in the world! Remember your affirmation "I AM AWESOME"!
2
1
3

J is for JOY. Every day we should wake up feeling joyful. Throughout the day, try to surround yourself with positive people. J is also for JOKE. Tell someone a joke today and make them laugh. Brighten up their day.

K
K is for KINDNESS. Kindness means being equally nice to everyone. It means being warm and generous. It's cool to be kind!
Help

L
L is for LOVE. We have to love ourselves first.
We need to put ourselves first and then we can love others.
Know that you are loved! L is also for LAUGH, a good
belly laugh is so good for you. Try it and see!!

M
M is for MINDFUL. Focus on the present moment.
Begin every day with positive affirmations.
You are magic! Life is magic! Believe it!

N is for NICE. If you are nice to others, you feel good about yourself. N is also for NO. It is OK to say No if we do not want to do something or if that feels wrong to you.

No

O is for OPTIMISTIC. This word means seeing the bright side of a situation or expecting good things to happen. Positive people generally feel optimistic about life. They expect good things to happen. Spread your happiness wherever you go!
Is this glass half full or half empty?

P
P is for PERSISTENCE. Do not give up on your goal. Focus and keep going! P is also for PLEASE. it's a good thing to have good manners. Don't forget to say please and thank you!
Please and thank yo

Q is for QUALITIES. What are your good qualities? List them out and write them down. Is kindness one of them? Think about someone you know who has good qualities! Do you like and admire this person?

R is for RADIANT. Radiant means to shine bright.
Show the world how your light inside shines.
You are radiant and bright! R is also for READY.
Make sure you are ready for school every day and
make your bed before you go!

S is for **SET GOALS.** Think about the results you want to see. Before you set a goal ask yourself what you want to achieve, write them down and take action. Reach for the stars!

T
T is for TRY. Say it with me "I always try my best". Watch out. Good things are coming your way. T is also for THINK. If you consciously think happy thoughts, you will be happy. Watch those thoughts, make sure they are good ones!
"I am thinking happy thoughts"
"I always try my best"

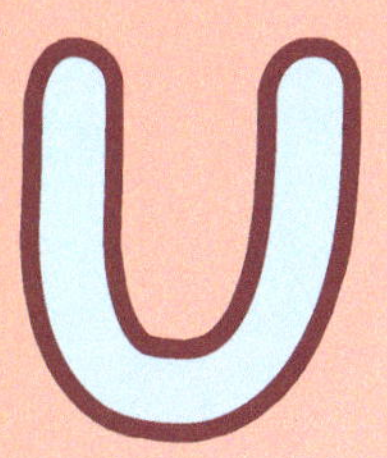

U is for UPBEAT. Try to stay upbeat.
Do something you love. Listen to your favourite
music or watch your favourite movie or TV programme or play
with your friends. Do something that makes you happy!

V
V is for VIP. You are a Very Important Person. A lot of people love and care about you. You are a VIP in a lot of people's lives. V is also for VISUALISE. Dare to Dream – visualise what you want and its magic – it might just come true!
VIP

W is for WRITE. I will tell you a big secret. If you write out or draw a picture of what you would really love and do that every day, it might just come true!

X
X is for X-RAY VISION. Do you have a goal?
How do you achieve that goal? Be a superhero like
Superman, he has X-ray vision and knows that helps him to
and to out there and save the day! X is also for XO.
Who doesn't love some hugs and kisses!

Y
Y is for YOU. Be yourself. Speak to yourself positively.
Believe in yourself! See the beauty in YOU!
Don't try to copy or be anyone else.

Z is for ZEST. Have you got a zest for life? Do you have a feeling of enjoyment and enthusiasm for life? If you use affirmations and visualisation every day, you will see your life improving every day! Z is also for ZERO. Give yourself a high five and remember how much you have grown since you were a little baby! You are AMAZING!